PRAYING GOD'S PROMISES FOR MY CHILD

PRAYING GOD'S PROMISES for MY CHILD

Linda K. Taylor

Tyndale House Publishers, Inc.
Wheaton, Illinois

Visit Tyndale's exciting Web site at www.tyndale.com

Praying God's Promises for My Child

Copyright © 2002 by Linda K. Taylor. All rights reserved.

Cover illustration by Julie Chen. Copyright © 2002 by Tyndale House Publishers. All rights reserved.

Designed by Julie Chen

Edited by Susan Taylor

Scripture quotations are taken from the *Holy Bible,* New Living Translation, copyright © 1996. Used by permission of Tyndale House Publishers, Inc., Wheaton, Illinois 60189. All rights reserved.

Library of Congress Cataloging-in-Publication Data

Taylor, Linda Chaffee, 1958-
    Praying God's promises for my child / Linda K. Taylor.
        p. cm.
Includes indexes.
    ISBN 0-8423-5608-8
    1. Parents—Prayer-books and devotions—English. 2. God—Promises—Prayer-books and
devotions—English. I. Title.
BV4845 . T38 2002
242'.645—dc21

2001008413

Printed in the United States of America

08 07 06 05 04 03 02
 7   6   5   4   3   2   1

TO MY PRECIOUS CHILDREN

COURTNEY

TOM

SEAN

OVER WHOM WE PRAY EVERY DAY.

His faithful promises are your armor

and protection.

Psalm 91:4

We have continued praying for you ever since we first

heard about you. We ask God to give you a complete

understanding of what he wants to do in your lives,

and we ask him to make you wise with spiritual wisdom.

Then the way you live will always honor and please

the Lord, and you will continually do good,

kind things for others. All the while,

you will learn to know God better and better.

Colossians 1:9-10

PART 1: PRAYING ABOUT MY CHILD'S CHOICES

Salvation and Spiritual Growth

Relationships

Times of Temptation

PART 2: PRAYING ABOUT MY CHILD'S CHARACTER

The Fruit of the Spirit

Living the Christian Life

PART 3: PRAYING ABOUT MY CHILD'S CHALLENGES

Times of Fear and Worry

Times of Trial

CONTENTS

THANKS TO SEVERAL VERY SPECIAL MOMS AND GRANDMOTHERS

WHO HELPED ME WITH VERSE REFERENCES, IDEAS,

AND ENCOURAGEMENT FOR THIS BOOK:

MY MOM, REVA CHAFFEE; MY SISTER, CAROL FIELDING;

LORETTA BIRCHARD, JENNY GORR, CINDY HESLINGA,

SHARON IRVIN, RUTH JACOBS, LINDA KRIER,

MICHELLE MORRIS, DEBBIE PREBBLE,

AND SHIRLEY WEBSTER.

Y O U are probably already praying regularly for your children. As Christian parents we know the power of prayer in our own lives, so we know its power for our children's lives. There is so much we want for our children—so many dreams, hopes, plans. Are we forgetting anything as we teach our children day by day? Is there some vital life skill or attitude or set of manners that we have accidentally skipped? How can we possibly get it all in? Eighteen years is a long time, but those years pass with barely a blink.

This book is meant merely to be a guide as you pray for your precious children. The topics are certainly not exhaustive; however, I have attempted to include many areas of life where I desire to cover my own children with prayer. A few prayers focus on praying for salvation. Many of them are appropriate for young children. Most can be prayed for your growing and grown children—but most of those prayers assume that your children have a relationship with Christ. If you have a child who doesn't know Christ yet, then certainly praying about that is the place to begin. So use these prayers as your own starting point. If you need some words, I have suggested some prayers. But in many cases you will want to say in your own words what is appropriate for whatever situation your child may be in.

What makes this book different from many of the other

prayer books available today? This book uses promises from God's Word as the basis for praying for our children. The Bible is filled with God's promises, and so I have sought to pray the reality of those promises into my children's lives.

It's important to note that some of the promises in Scripture were made to the nation of Israel—God's chosen people. Because we are believers, we can appropriate the truth of many of those promises even though they were not directed specifically to us. However, we need to be careful to look at the context of the specific portion of Scripture and take that into account as we take hold of God's promises. Other verses are promises that declare God's character. We can claim them as promises because the unchanging nature and trustworthiness of God's character naturally flow into the unchanging nature and reliability of his words to us. In addition, many verses come from the book of Proverbs. Here again, we need to consider the context of the book: Proverbs are general truths, not necessarily promises. In these cases, we can pray that these general principles will be true in our children's lives!

And, of course, we must always take into account God's grace. A key to that grace is his granting us the ability to choose. While our children are young, we make many choices for them. As you pray these promises for your young children, be sure that you are also teaching and modeling the concepts that you pray about. Prayer does not absolve us from our responsibility to teach, train, discipline, and guide.

If you are praying for adult children, remember that God grants them freedom to choose also. Praying God's promises is not some kind of magic formula that will fix their lives. Your prayers for your children have great power, but you must always trust God to work in his way and in his time. Be patient. If you must keep praying for years, then keep praying for years. In fact, you may not see the answer in your lifetime. But keep praying. Sometimes that is the most powerful thing you can do.

PART ONE

PRAYING ABOUT MY CHILD'S CHOICES

ONE of the greatest gifts our heavenly Father gave us was the gift of choice. However, it can be a painful gift as well, for along with the ability to choose comes the opportunity to choose wrongly. How many times in my own life I have had the choice, gone in the wrong direction, and regretted it. But I also remember many times when two paths stood before me like a fork in the road, and as I sought God's guidance, I clearly felt the nudge to go a certain way. At the time the reasons for a particular choice were not crystal clear, but I *knew* that God was guiding me. There can be no greater joy than to have the choice, trust in the Guide, follow his lead, and discover what he has planned along the way!

Our children will face many choices. From the time they are old enough to say no, they are old enough to make choices. As parents, we seek to train and guide them in making the best choices. We give them skills for decision making, teach them common sense, and offer them advice and the benefit of our experience to guide them. As we do those things, we must also pray that those skills will carry them through the many choices that lie ahead.

Of course, our children's most important choice will be to accept Jesus Christ as their Lord and Savior—and we pray for that. Then we pray that their relationship with Christ will guide their spiritual walk and help them choose the path God has for them.

THE PROMISE
THOSE WHO BELIEVE WILL BE SAVED

If you confess with your mouth that Jesus is Lord and believe in your heart that God raised him from the dead, you will be saved. For it is by believing in your heart that you are made right with God, and it is by confessing with your mouth that you are saved.   Romans 10:9-10

IF your child is not a believer, you are surely hurting. Perhaps you only recently became a believer yourself, so you didn't bring up your child in the faith you now profess. Perhaps you think you did everything wrong and now you are punishing yourself. Or maybe your child was at church with you every time the doors were open, and now he is rebelling, trying to "find his own way." Perhaps you think you did everything right, and you can't believe this is happening.

Whether we think we did wrong or right, we need not punish ourselves or wonder what we could or should have done better. We will be far better off spending our energy on our knees in fervent prayer for our children. Children need to find faith for themselves. Every child needs to make it personal. God works in every child in a different way. But God promises that every person who believes and confesses Jesus as Lord will be saved. We can pray that our children will come to the point of realizing that this is the only way to true life and peace. Remember, we can't do it *for* them. The Holy Spirit must work *in* them.

PRAYING GOD'S PROMISE

Dear God, you promise that those who believe in Jesus and confess him as Lord will be saved. Lord, I pray that my child will see his need for you. I pray that he will call upon you. Please guide him toward confession and belief. I understand that this may mean some difficulty in my child's life before he gets to that point. But please work in his life in whatever way you need to in order to help him confess with his mouth that Jesus is Lord and believe in his heart that you raised Jesus from the dead. Make me a good example to my child as I live my life for you.

GOD'S PROMISE TO YOU

- God will save those who confess and believe.
- By believing in God, your child will be made right with him.
- By confessing his faith in God, your child will be saved.

THE PROMISE
GOD FREES US FROM SIN

We are made right in God's sight when we trust in Jesus Christ to take away our sins. And we all can be saved in this same way, no matter who we are or what we have done. For all have sinned; all fall short of God's glorious standard. Yet now God in his gracious kindness declares us not guilty. He has done this through Christ Jesus, who has freed us by taking away our sins.   Romans 3:22-24

WHAT a glorious promise! God loves us so much that he wanted to make us right with him. Because he is a just God, he could not simply overlook sin. His justice required that someone pay the penalty for our sin. And someone did! God sent his only Son as the perfect sacrifice to take the punishment our sins deserved.

God promises that when we trust in what Jesus did for us, he will take away our sins—no matter who we are or what we have done. No sin is so great that God cannot wipe it away. Now, because of Jesus' death, God declares us not guilty and sets us free. Of course, we will never be completely without sin until we get to heaven, but in the meantime, God looks at us and sees Christ's righteousness instead of our sin. "Gracious kindness" indeed! We must pray that our children will ask Christ to take away their sins. No matter what our children have done, Christ can set them free!

PRAYING GOD'S PROMISE

You say, Lord, that we are made right in your sight when we trust in your Son to take away our sins. I pray that my child will trust Jesus Christ as her Savior. I pray that the moment will come when your Spirit will speak to her heart and help her to see her need for you. I thank you for the promise that when she trusts in you to take away her sins, she will be made right in your sight. You say that salvation is found only in Jesus Christ and we need only to trust in him and he will take away our sins. I pray that my child will understand this and be willing to come to you, no matter what she has done. Lord, set my child free—from the sins that entangle her, the problems that cloud her vision, the stubbornness that won't relent, the fear that won't subside, the addictions that won't let go. You are more powerful than all of these things. May my child find true freedom in Jesus Christ.

GOD'S PROMISE TO YOU

- Your child is made right in God's sight when she trusts in his Son to take away her sins. When she does, God will declare her not guilty.
- By accepting Christ's sacrifice, your child will be set free.

THE PROMISE
GOD REWARDS THOSE WHO SEEK HIM

It is impossible to please God without faith. Anyone who wants to come to him must believe that there is a God and that he rewards those who sincerely seek him.   Hebrews 11:6

PEOPLE may try all kinds of things in an attempt to please God. Many think that just going to church will do it. Some try just being generous and kind, living a good life, or keeping all kinds of rules. But the Bible makes it clear that it is impossible to please God without faith. In other words, all of our "doing" amounts to nothing. We can attend church, give our money, serve others, and flawlessly keep all kinds of rules we set for ourselves, but if we do not have faith in God, we cannot please him.

Our children need to know that God wants their faith to be personal and sincere. When we have true biblical faith, we believe in God and his goodness. We come to him believing that he exists and, even more, believing that God rewards those who search for him. Jesus said, "Keep on asking, and you will be given what you ask for. Keep on looking, and you will find. Keep on knocking, and the door will be opened" (Matthew 7:7). God rewards us with himself and his presence forever. It's a very simple process. Anyone, anytime, anywhere can come, believe, and receive. It's a simple process—with eternal rewards.

PRAYING GOD'S PROMISE

Lord, you say that it is impossible to please you without faith, and so, Lord, I pray that my child will come to faith in you. I pray that he will understand the importance of a personal relationship with you, based not on his works but on his faith. You say that anyone who wants to come to you must believe that you exist. Draw my child to you and help him to sincerely believe in your existence as an almighty yet loving God. I pray that as he sincerely seeks you, you will show yourself to him. Draw my child to you, dear Lord, for you are the greatest reward of all.

GOD'S PROMISE TO YOU

- It is impossible to please God without faith.
- Your child can come to God by believing that he exists and that he rewards those who sincerely seek him.

THE PROMISE
GOD GIVES US ETERNAL LIFE

All who believe in God's Son have eternal life. Those who don't obey the Son will never experience eternal life, but the wrath of God remains upon them.   John 3:36

It doesn't get much clearer than this. God promises eternal life to those who believe; he promises his eternal wrath to those who live in unbelief and disobedience. There are only two choices. We either believe Jesus is who he said he is, or we don't. We either choose to follow him, or we don't. As C. S. Lewis wrote in *Mere Christianity,* "You must make your choice. Either this man was, and is, the Son of God: or else a madman or something worse. . . . But let us not come with any patronizing nonsense about His being a great human teacher. He has not left that open to us. He did not intend to."

The choice is clear; the promise is clear. John repeated the sentiment in another book: "Whoever has God's Son has life; whoever does not have his Son does not have life. I write this to you who believe in the Son of God, so that you may know you have eternal life" (1 John 5:12-13). He wrote so that we could *know* that we have eternal life—not *hope* that we have it but *know* it. People may attempt to derail our children's faith or plant seeds of doubt in their hearts, so we need to pray that our children will believe and *know* that they have eternal life.

PRAYING GOD'S PROMISE

Lord, you promise that all who believe in your Son have eternal life. Thank you for that promise. I pray that my child will believe in you, Jesus. I ask that she will believe that you are who you say you are—the Savior of the world. You promise that we can know that we have eternal life. I pray that after confessing belief in you, my child will be kept from doubts and will be certain of her eternity with you. May that promise bring my child joy every day of her life.

GOD'S PROMISE TO YOU

- Any child who believes in Jesus will have eternal life.
- Your child never needs to doubt God's promise to give her eternal life when she believes.

THE PROMISE
GOD BLESSES HIS PEOPLE

Who may climb the mountain of the Lord? Who may stand in his holy place? Only those whose hands and hearts are pure, who do not worship idols and never tell lies. They will receive the Lord's blessing and have right standing with God their savior. They alone may enter God's presence and worship the God of Israel.   Psalm 24:3-6

As parents, we pray that our children will belong to God. We want them to be among those who can "climb the mountain of the Lord" and "stand in his holy place." When the Israelites sang this psalm, possibly every Sabbath in the worship services at the temple, they were acknowledging God's holiness and their need to be pure before him.

In our own strength, none of us can be totally clean, perfect, and acceptable to God. If that were true, Christ would not have had to die. We must pray that our children will accept the sacrifice of Christ and so receive the gift of the Holy Spirit. As the Holy Spirit works in our children, they will be able to turn from idolatry, stay pure, and have truthful speech. The glorious promise is that our children will "receive the Lord's blessing and have right standing with God their savior." Then they are welcomed into God's presence. What more could a parent want?

PRAYING GOD'S PROMISE

Oh Lord, I pray that my child will desire to be in your presence and to have a personal relationship with you. You desire that your people's hands and hearts be pure, that your children not worship idols or tell lies. May the Holy Spirit work in my child's heart so that he will be kept pure. I pray that his hands—work, service, and actions—will always be pure before you. I pray that his heart— relationships, motives, and desires—will always be pure before you. Help my child to never let anything become more important to him than you are, for that would be idolatry. Lord, help my child to be a person of the truth and a person of truthfulness. Lord, you promise that such people will receive your blessing and have right standing before you. Thank you, Lord, for offering your blessing to my child. I pray that he will always desire to walk with you and so enter into your presence with awe and worship.

GOD'S PROMISE TO YOU

- God gives blessing and right standing to those who accept Christ's sacrifice and seek to follow the Holy Spirit's leading.
- The child who trusts in God will be welcome in his presence.

THE PROMISE
GOD PREPARES AND EQUIPS US

All Scripture is inspired by God and is useful to teach us what is true and to make us realize what is wrong in our lives. It straightens us out and teaches us to do what is right. It is God's way of preparing us in every way, fully equipped for every good thing God wants us to do.   2 Timothy 3:16-17

SOME of my children's favorite books include *Anne of Green Gables*, *Charlotte's Web*, and *The Lion, the Witch, and the Wardrobe*. With all the reading we do, I'm also working on helping them to see the Bible as their ultimate favorite book. I want them to understand that the Bible is God's letter to them, that it is the source of God's voice and his answers to their prayers, and that it offers guidance for every choice and decision they will ever have to make.

We can begin by helping our children see that the Bible is not a big, scary, overwhelming book. They need to understand that the Bible is the story of salvation from beginning to end. It tells us why we need salvation, how God provided it, and what we must do about it. By teaching and by example, we can give our children the tools to know how to read God's Word for themselves. If your child doesn't have a Bible, find one at her age level and get started reading. Help her to see the Bible as a comfortable and familiar book. In time, maybe it will even become her favorite!

PRAYING GOD'S PROMISE

Oh Lord, thank you for giving us your Word, the Bible, in such a wonderful way. I pray that my child will understand its value, enjoy reading it, and learn how to apply its truths to her daily life. Lord God, you say that the Bible is useful to teach the truth, to show where we have gone wrong, to straighten us out, and to teach us to do what is right. I pray that my child will hear you speaking to her through it. Reveal your truth, point out if there is anything wrong in her life, make her open to your teaching. You promise that your Word will fully equip us for every good thing you want us to do. Please use your Word to prepare and equip my child for the service to which you have called her.

GOD'S PROMISE TO YOU

- God's Word teaches truth and will help your child realize what is wrong in her life.
- His Word can straighten out your child's life and teach her what is right.
- God's Word prepares and equips your child to do whatever he wants her to do for him.

THE PROMISE
WE CAN TRUST GOD

Those who know your name trust in you, for you, O Lord, have never abandoned anyone who searches for you.

Psalm 9:10

WHAT does it mean to trust someone? Webster's says that it means we can rely on his integrity, strength, ability, or surety. When we trust someone, we have confidence in that person; we know that we can rely on him.

Today's verse tells us that those who know God trust him. We can rely on his integrity, strength, and ability; we have confidence in him. He has shown us his trustworthiness through his Word, in the lives of other people, and in our own lives. The promise is that God never abandons anyone who searches for him.

Is your child searching today? Is he questioning? asking? rebelling? tossing your beliefs back in your face? doubting? looking for God in the wrong places? People's searches will send them in many different directions, and that can make us afraid for our children. We must pray that God will not abandon those who are seeking him. Pray that your child's search will lead him back to God.

PRAYING GOD'S PROMISE

You promise, Lord, that you have never abandoned anyone who searches for you. My child is searching today, Lord. I know that I have the answer, but he wants to seek it out for himself. I know that can be a good thing, Lord, but it is also scary for me. I fear that he will go in the wrong direction, fall into wrong teaching, or spurn his faith completely. Thank you for your promise that you will not abandon my child in his search. I ask that it will lead him directly back to you.

GOD'S PROMISE TO YOU

- God knows that your child is searching, and he knows why.
- He will not abandon your child in his search.

THE PROMISE
WE CAN LIVE GODLY LIVES

As we know Jesus better, his divine power gives us everything we need for living a godly life. He has called us to receive his own glory and goodness! And by that same mighty power, he has given us all of his rich and wonderful promises. . . . So make every effort to apply the benefits of these promises to your life. Then your faith will produce a life of moral excellence.

2 Peter 1:3-5

LIVING a godly life sounds difficult and intimidating, doesn't it? After all, we're so imperfect! We can be glad that God promises that *we* don't have to do it alone; Jesus' divine power will give us everything we need to live godly lives. We don't need to keep an exhausting number of rules or lock ourselves away from the world. That is not God's plan. Instead, we are to draw upon the divine power Jesus gives us.

Peter goes on to say that Jesus' divine power also gives us all the promises of God's Word. If God's power gives God's promises, then those promises are sure and steadfast. As we apply the benefits of those promises to our lives, we can live with "moral excellence."

Where does it all begin? With "know[ing] Jesus better." We need to pray for spiritual growth for our children. We need to pray that they will want to know Jesus better and grow closer to him. As they do this, many rich and wonderful promises are theirs. Then, as they learn to apply these promises, their faith will produce lives of moral excellence. Now there's a prayer I want to pray for my children.

PRAYING GOD'S PROMISE

You promise, Lord, that as we get to know Jesus better, his divine power will give us everything we need for living a godly life. I pray that my child would desire to know you better and better. I pray that your divine power will give my child everything she needs to live a godly life. Thank you for giving my child your own glory and goodness. Help her to grow spiritually so that she will live for you. You say that your own power, Lord, has given us all your rich and wonderful promises and that as we apply these promises, our faith will produce lives of moral excellence. Oh Lord, I desire that my child will live a life of moral excellence. Help her to apply the benefits of all your promises to her life.

GOD'S PROMISE TO YOU

- God's power will give your child everything she needs to live a godly life.
- As your child applies God's promises to her life, her faith will produce a life of moral excellence.

THE PROMISE
WE CAN FIND TRUE LIFE

Jesus said to the disciples, "If any of you wants to be my follower, you must put aside your selfish ambition, shoulder your cross, and follow me. If you try to keep your life for yourself, you will lose it. But if you give up your life for me, you will find true life."   Matthew 16:24-25

THE crux of the Good News seems at first glance to be a contradiction: To follow our Lord and Savior, we must shoulder his cross. To find true life, we must be willing to lose our lives. God specializes in taking what makes sense to us and turning it upside down!

Confessing our belief in Christ as our Savior is only the first step. After we have done that, God calls us to *follow* Christ. That means that we must do as he did and go where he went. It doesn't mean that we spend our life in Israel as an itinerant preacher, but it does require that we set aside every selfish goal and desire and seek first what God wants for us. This attitude transforms self-centeredness into God-centeredness. To shoulder our cross means that we obey no matter what, even to the point of death.

Before they can grow spiritually, our children need to be followers of Jesus. We can pray that they will set aside selfish desires in order to seek God's best. We can pray that they will understand the cost of following Christ and be willing to pay it. As they give up their lives in order to be used by God, they will find true life. That's a promise.

PRAYING GOD'S PROMISE

Lord, you say that your followers need to set aside their selfish ambition and shoulder their cross. Help my child to always seek your very best, to set aside selfish ambitions and desires, and to trust that you have something far better in mind. Lord, you promise that if we give up our lives for you, we will find true life. I humbly pray that my own life will be an example of commitment to you, Lord. You promise that those who give up their lives for you will find the life that you have for them, one of complete fulfillment. I pray that my child will give up everything to follow you. There can be no better way to live.

GOD'S PROMISE TO YOU

- When your child gives up everything to follow God, he will not be disappointed.
- As your child lives for Christ, he will find true life.

THE PROMISE
GOD TRANSFORMS US

Don't copy the behavior and customs of this world, but let God transform you into a new person by changing the way you think. Then you will know what God wants you to do, and you will know how good and pleasing and perfect his will really is.   Romans 12:2

M Y children have asked me at various times, "How will I know what God wants me to do?" Many times over the course of my own life I have asked, "How can I know the will of God?" As I look back across thirty years with Jesus, I can see that a steady walk with God, seeking to follow him with small steps of faith, has transformed my life. The small steps brought me to the big goals. The quivering steps of faith kept me on solid foundations.

So how will your children know the will of God? Tell them to take the daily little steps. God never puts on the "high beams" and shows us the entire path ahead. We probably couldn't handle that anyway! Instead, he promises that his Word will be a lamp to light our feet, lighting up just a small portion of the path ahead (Psalm 119:105). Teach your children to walk in God's will today, to be different from the world by their faith, and to ask God to transform them as they learn more about him. Then they will be staying on the right path, taking small steps in the right direction, and doing God's "good and pleasing and perfect" will.

PRAYING GOD'S PROMISE

My child wants to know your will, Lord. Help her to grow closer to you, to understand the difference between what you desire and what the world offers. Teach her not to copy the behaviors and customs of this world but to be transformed into a new person. You promise that we can know your will as we are transformed by you. Change the way my child thinks, Lord. Help her to have the mind of Christ in all situations. Help her to study your Word so that she has the lamp that lights the path ahead. Give her the peace that comes from knowing your good, pleasing, and perfect will.

GOD'S PROMISE TO YOU

- God will transform your child into a new person as she seeks to follow him.
- He will let your child know his perfect will as she walks with him.

MANY relationships dot the landscape of our lives. We have a relationship with our friend Jesus Christ, who loved us so much that he died for us. We have relationships with family members, with fellow believers, and with unbelievers in our neighborhood, school, workplace, and community.

Our children need to be able to build positive relationships. They need to know how to relate to others, how to hold a conversation, how to be respectful, how to live honorably. They need to be able to build strong marriages. They need to know how to relate to unbelievers without violating God's command not to be unequally yoked. They need to know how to relate to fellow believers, who can sometimes be a very frustrating lot.

We need to pray that our children will choose positive relationships that will make life pleasant, rich, exciting, and enjoyable. We can also pray that they avoid negative relationships that will cause stress, sorrow, and difficulty. Ask God to give your children the wisdom to choose and build positive relationships that honor him.

THE PROMISE
WE ARE GOD'S FRIENDS

[Jesus said,] "I command you to love each other in the same way that I love you. And here is how to measure it—the greatest love is shown when people lay down their lives for their friends. You are my friends if you obey me. I no longer call you servants, because a master doesn't confide in his servants. Now you are my friends, since I have told you everything the Father told me."

John 15:12-15

JESUS is our friend. That's a thought that, if we give it some time, can truly blow our minds! Jesus, the glorious God of the universe, took on a frail human body, walked on the earth, faced ridicule and rejection, and was murdered by the people he had created. He faced pain and suffering because he loved us. He laid down his life. Why? So we could be his friends.

The most important relationship our children will ever have is their relationship with Jesus Christ. As with any friendship, it takes good communication and spending time together if the relationship is to grow. We can pray that our children's relationship with Christ will be a "best friend" relationship, that our children will love him, spend time alone with him, and talk to him daily. When our children are best friends with Jesus, they will have all the tools they need to be able to love others as much as Jesus loves them. To love sacrificially, to love when that love is not returned, to love even the unlovable—that is Jesus' kind of love. That's what friendship with Jesus can do for your child's relationships.

PRAYING GOD'S PROMISE

Lord, you command us as believers to love one another as you have loved us. You exemplified that love when you died for us. I pray that you will help my child to follow your command to love others with your kind of love. Lord, as your followers we are also your friends. Help my child to see you as his best friend, Lord. I pray that he will take time every day to be with you—to read your Word and listen for your voice, to communicate with you, to seek your guidance. That friendship will provide the ability for him to do all that you desire—including loving others. Thank you for the great gift of your friendship, Lord. Keep my child from taking it for granted, and please continue to build that friendship throughout his life.

GOD'S PROMISE TO YOU

- God loved your child so much that he died for him.
- Your child can be God's friend.

THE PROMISE
GOD BLESSES US WHEN WE OBEY OUR PARENTS

Children, obey your parents because you belong to the Lord, for
this is the right thing to do. "Honor your father and mother."
This is the first of the Ten Commandments that ends with a
promise. And this is the promise: If you honor your father and
mother, "you will live a long life, full of blessing."

Ephesians 6:1-3

OKAY, so we parents like to throw the weight of this verse
around with our children: "See, it says *obey* your parents! And
see, one of the Ten Commandments says to *honor* your parents."
The reality is that this is important stuff and our children
should take notice. Paul noted that the command to honor
one's parents ends with a promise directly from God—that
those who do "will live a long life, full of blessing."

Of course, our children's motivation for obedience is rarely
to live a long life or to get truckloads of blessing. Instead, the
point is that as children obey their parents, they are learning an
attitude of respect that will carry over into their relationship
with God. In addition, as they obey their parents, they will be
kept safe from harm—thus paving the way for a long, full life.

Children are to obey and honor their parents. They are not
merely to do as they are told but are to respect and esteem their
parents. Our children may not always agree with us, but they

can always be respectful—and that is what we must teach them. And as parents we must be good examples by demonstrating a respectable and honorable manner in our interaction with our children and with others.

PRAYING GOD'S PROMISE

Lord, you promise that children who obey and honor their parents will be greatly blessed. Sometimes I get so tired, Lord; I want my child to obey and to be respectful, and it's a full-time job guiding her to do that. But I want the promise for my child, Lord. I want her to receive the blessings that result from your commandment. Help me as I teach and guide my child, Lord. Help me to be respectable and to require respect. Help me to be wise in the obedience I require and in the discipline I give for disobedience.

GOD'S PROMISE TO YOU

- God will bless your child when she obeys and honors you.
- He will help you to be a wise and discerning parent.

THE PROMISE
A SPOUSE CAN BE A TREASURE

The man who finds a wife finds a treasure and receives favor
from the Lord.   Proverbs 18:22

As an avid reader, I read every Christian child-rearing book I
could find when Tom and I managed to have three children in
the span of thirty-three months. I knew I needed help! I remember
vividly the time I discovered that I could begin praying
about my children's future spouses from the time they were
babies. What a concept! Given the challenges of marriage, it
seems of great value to begin now to cover my children, the
spouses God may give them, and their marriages in prayer.

The proverb says that "the man who finds a wife finds a treasure
and receives favor from the Lord." Of course, proverbs are
just that—general truths. Although we can't technically call
them promises, we can pray that the general truth *will* be true
for our children! We can pray that if it is God's will that our
children marry, he will give them wisdom, discernment, and a
willingness to listen carefully to his guidance. We can pray that
our sons will find wives who will be "treasures" to them and
that they will be godly husbands. We can pray that our daughters
will find godly husbands to whom they will be priceless
treasures.

PRAYING GOD'S PROMISE

Lord, you know how tough marriage can be! In fact, the world doesn't often give us the picture of spouses truly "treasuring" one another and receiving your favor. I pray for my child, Lord. If it is your will that he not marry, please help him to accept that, understanding that you will bless him for following your will. If he does marry, may your hand be evident in that relationship. The proverb speaks of treasures and of your favor. I want only what is best for my child, Lord; and I know that's what you want as well. Guide my child to the spouse you have prepared, a spouse who will be as great a find as a priceless treasure.

GOD'S PROMISE TO YOU

- Marriage has God's stamp of approval, and he can help your child's marriage be a great success.
- He can help your child be a treasure to his spouse—and he can help the spouse to see it!

their lives through the presence of his Holy Spirit. Then our children's lives will bring much glory and praise to God.

PRAYING GOD'S PROMISE

Lord, the words in today's verse sound like what I want to say to my child every day. You say that you want us to understand what really matters and to live pure and blameless lives until you return. I pray that my child will grow spiritually and that you will help her to understand what really matters in life. I pray that she will not be caught up in chasing after what doesn't matter but instead will focus on her relationship with you and on growing more like you. Help her to live a pure and blameless life in every area. You promise that as your people are filled with the fruit of the Spirit, it will bring you much glory and praise. May my child be a source of glory and praise for you, dear Lord. I pray that your Spirit will so fill her with luscious, ripened fruit that you will receive great honor.

GOD'S PROMISE TO YOU

- Through a relationship with Christ your child can understand what really matters and can live a pure and blameless life.
- God will receive much glory and praise when the fruit of his Spirit grows and ripens in your child's life.

RECEIVING Jesus Christ is just the beginning of a lifetime of adventure with him. The word *justification* means having right standing with God because of Christ's sacrifice on our behalf.

God could take us right to heaven the moment we believe, but he chooses instead to leave us here on this earth. Why? Well, this earth provides plenty of situations to test and grow our faith. That's what *sanctification* is all about. It is a process of walking daily with Christ and learning how to obey him in the various situations of our lives. We are not trying in our own power to become perfect; instead, we are walking with Christ and asking his Holy Spirit to work in our lives and make us Christlike.

Let's pray for our children to learn what it means to walk with Christ moment by moment. May they learn what it means to live their faith, to "walk the talk." May they see that this is truly the best way to live!

THE PROMISE
GOD MAKES US NEW PEOPLE

[Christ] died for everyone so that those who receive his new life will no longer live to please themselves. Instead, they will live to please Christ, who died and was raised for them. . . . What this means is that those who become Christians become new persons. They are not the same anymore, for the old life is gone. A new life has begun! 2 Corinthians 5:15-17

JESUS Christ died for everyone—not just for a few people, not just for the good people or the teachable people, but for everyone. He died for you; he died for me; he died for our children. In light of his death to take the punishment for our sins, we should no longer live to please ourselves. That's not what life is all about. With Christ, we have a new reason for being, a new focus in living. He has made us "new persons." The old life is gone, and a new life has begun.

When our children become believers, they are new people with new lives. What a joyous thought! Do they still have to face down their old nature? Of course, but with Christ they can be victorious. Is there spiritual warfare? Yes, and Christ can prepare them for battle. Does Christ live in them to make their lives all that he wants them to be? Most surely! Praise God for making us new people with new lives. That's what living the Christian life is all about—living victoriously for Jesus!

PRAYING GOD'S PROMISE

You died, Jesus, so that those who receive you will no longer live for themselves but will live for you. Work in my child's heart to receive you if he hasn't already, Lord. You promise that those who receive you become new people with new lives and a new nature. You call your people not to live for selfish pleasure but to please you. And you give us your Holy Spirit to help us to do that. I'm so thankful that you don't leave us alone to figure this out, Lord. I praise you, Lord, that you offer to save my beloved child, to make him a new person, and give him a new life. You offer him a life of joy, victory, and fulfillment! As my child seeks to live for you, help him to understand that this is not a life of drudgery but one of joyous service to you!

GOD'S PROMISE TO YOU

- Christ died so that your child could live to please God.
- When your child puts his faith in Christ, he becomes a new person. He is not the same anymore; a new life has begun!

THE PROMISE
WE CAN LIVE BY FAITH

I have been crucified with Christ. I myself no longer live, but Christ lives in me. So I live my life in this earthly body by trusting in the Son of God, who loved me and gave himself for me.   Galatians 2:19-20

T H E S E verses have sort of a mystical wonder to them. If we try to wrap our minds around these concepts, we can give ourselves a brain freeze! We have been crucified, yet we live. We died, and yet we are alive. We are still ourselves living our lives, but Christ is living in and through us. In these words is the breathless wonder of our intimate relationship with Jesus Christ. He is not a god "out there" somewhere; he is not a stone-cold idol. He is a person who lived, died, and rose again. He is God himself, brought into focus before our eyes. When we accept him as our Savior, his crucifixion becomes our own, for he was crucified in our place. Now, through his Holy Spirit, he lives in us, and we live our lives by faith in him, trusting the One who loved us and gave himself for us.

Let's pray that our children will sense the wonder of what Christ has done for them. May they sense the glory of being crucified and raised with Christ and resolve to live out their faith in him.

PRAYING GOD'S PROMISE

We have been crucified with Christ, and so we no longer live, but he lives in us. What a wonder it is, Lord, that you would take up residence in our lives! I ask that my child will sense this same wonder. What a glorious promise to know that you will live in my child and give her a new life. Your Word says that we live by faith in you, Lord. As you live in my child, Lord, I pray that she will be set free, as Paul was, to serve you with all her heart and soul. May she live joyously because of her faith in you.

GOD'S PROMISE TO YOU

- Because God is loving, he gave his Son so your child could know him and become a new person with a new life.

THE PROMISE
WE ARE CHRIST'S WITNESSES

Jesus came and told his disciples, "I have been given complete authority in heaven and on earth. Therefore, go and make disciples of all the nations, baptizing them in the name of the Father and the Son and the Holy Spirit. Teach these new disciples to obey all the commands I have given you. And be sure of this: I am with you always, even to the end of the age."

Matthew 28:18-20

THERE'S no doubt about the job Jesus left for us to do. He did not say, "Go hide away from this evil world and keep clear of its influence." He didn't say, "Don't get near those nasty unbelievers who do such sinful things!" He said, "Go and make disciples of all the nations." It sounds to me as if that means stepping out of our comfort zones—whether across the street or around the world—to find people who need to know Christ. Besides, we were once part of those "nasty unbelievers," and they are the ones who need to hear the message!

Our children will encounter plenty of unbelievers as they grow up, first in school, in the neighborhood, on the playground, and then at college, in the workplace, through community involvements. Throughout their lives, there will be plenty of places in their "world" where people need to be reached. Whether God calls your children to live on the other side of the globe or to have an impact in their school or workplace, they need to gain a heart for the lost so that they can do as Christ commands and "make disciples." As parents, we need to be examples in our concern for the lost and our witness to the people God has placed in our sphere of influence.

PRAYING GOD'S PROMISE

Jesus, help me to be a good example to my child about concern for the lost. I want my child to see that your command is not just for missionaries across the globe; it is also for him as he reaches out to his friends. As my child grows in his faith, give him a heart of concern that prays for the lost in his school, in the neighborhood, or in the workplace. In words, deeds, and attitudes may my child stand out in the crowd as one who has found the answer to life! You promise, Lord, to be with us always, even to the end of the age. That promise of your continuous presence in my child's life gives me great peace, Lord, for I know that wherever you call him, you will be with him.

GOD'S PROMISE TO YOU

- Through God's power your child can be a part of making disciples of all nations.
- Jesus is with your child always, even to the end of time.

THE PROMISE
OUR THOUGHT PATTERNS CAN CHANGE

> Dear brothers and sisters, let me say one more thing as I close this letter. Fix your thoughts on what is true and honorable and right. Think about things that are pure and lovely and admirable. Think about things that are excellent and worthy of praise. Keep putting into practice all you learned from me and heard from me and saw me doing, and the God of peace will be with you.
>
> Philippians 4:8-9

Do you have days when you feel completely out of control? I do. My mind focuses on everything that's wrong with my life: my house, my body, my abilities. I feel as if I can't do anything right.

On those days in particular I really need these verses from Philippians. I need to fix my thoughts on what is true and honorable and right, not on what is false, undignified, or unrighteous. On those difficult days, there is very little about my thoughts that is pure, lovely, admirable, excellent, or praiseworthy. How easy it can be to fall into the haze of self-pity. Instead, I need to "fix" my thoughts and "think about" what I'm thinking about! After all, I would like to tell my kids that they can put into practice all that they "learned from me and heard from me and saw me doing." But on some days that could be downright dangerous if I don't watch what I think about! With

God's help, I can have fewer and fewer of those days. Let's pray that our children will be able to think about things that are "excellent and worthy of praise."

PRAYING GOD'S PROMISE

Our thought patterns have such a strong effect on our lives, Lord. You have told us, Jesus, that sin begins with thoughts. Give my child the ability to think as you think, Lord, so that she will be able to dwell on what is true, honorable, and right. Help her to have thoughts that are pure, wholesome, lovely, and pleasing to you. Paul told his readers to put into practice what they had learned and heard from him and seen him doing. Help me with my own thought patterns so that I, too, can develop the mind of Christ. I want to be able to tell my child to follow my example, Lord. Work through my weakness, Lord, so that she may see you in me.

GOD'S PROMISE TO YOU

- When your child fixes her thoughts on positive things, she can avoid much sin.

THE PROMISE
WE CAN HAVE JOY IN TROUBLES

Dear brothers and sisters, whenever trouble comes your way, let it be an opportunity for joy. For when your faith is tested, your endurance has a chance to grow. So let it grow, for when your endurance is fully developed, you will be strong in character and ready for anything.   James 1:2-4

BELIEVERS should be unmistakably identified as people who have an amazing outlook on their troubles. Think about it—

- we have the Holy Spirit in our hearts,
- we know that God promises to work all things together for good,
- we know that God knows the future,
- we know that anything that happens to us is allowed by him for a purpose, and
- we know that he wants us to grow to maturity.

The troubles that come into our lives should not surprise us, make us doubt God's love for us, or put us into a tailspin. Instead, our response should be joy. No, we don't have to be happy about the trouble, but we can graciously accept what God has allowed to happen because we know that he has a good purpose for it. And yes, troubles test our faith, but tested faith results in endurance. And as endurance grows, we gain spiritual maturity.

Troubles are inevitable. How we handle them shows our true colors. Pray that your children will be able to face troubles with joy and so gain endurance and strong character.

PRAYING GOD'S PROMISE

Lord, one hallmark of our faith should be our ability to face troubles with your perspective in mind. Give my child the ability to face troubles with your grace. I pray that with each trouble that comes into my child's life, you will teach him how to have joy, the deep inner joy that nothing can take away. May he understand that this experience is like the "growing pains" he had as a child. The pains mean that we are growing. You promise that when our faith is tested, endurance has a chance to grow. Then endurance will build strong character and make us ready for anything. Give my child endurance through his trials and troubles. Give him an awesome sense of your presence and of your good plan for his life. As his faith is tested, may he pass with flying colors! Through the trials he must face, grow strong character in him so that he is ready for anything.

GOD'S PROMISE TO YOU

- Troubles and trials can be an opportunity for joy.
- When your child's faith is tested, God will teach him endurance and produce maturity and strength of character. Then your child will be ready for anything.

THE PROMISE
WE HAVE POWER

God has not given us a spirit of fear and timidity, but of power, love, and self-discipline.   2 Timothy 1:7

GOD has not called Christians to be fearful, cowering doormats waiting to let the world step on our faith and wipe its feet on our principles. With the God of the universe in our hearts, we have a spirit of power, love, and self-discipline. Paul wrote the words in today's verse to Timothy, a young man with a big responsibility as pastor of the church in Ephesus.

People in leadership need God's help. Wherever we lead, God promises *power*—boldness to speak the truth. We don't have this power in order to lord it over others but to empower them, to give them boldness in their faith as well. God promises *love,* a fruit of the Spirit. We have power to speak the truth, but love for our listeners tempers that power so it does not become prideful. God also promises *self-discipline,* or self-control, which gives us a cool head and a sound perspective in the hazards of leadership.

Our children will eventually begin to move into leadership in their homes, churches, communities, and businesses. Pray that they will not be fearful and timid but will have the spirit of power, love, and self-discipline as they lead.

PRAYING GOD'S PROMISE

Leadership is a big responsibility, Lord. I pray for my child in her leadership responsibilities. No leader can please everyone, and every leader eventually needs to take a stand on important issues. So I pray that my child will be strong in her faith and able to stand on her principles. You promise that you do not give us a spirit of fear and timidity but of power, love, and self-discipline. Give my child power and boldness without pride. Give my child the grace to speak the truth from loving motives. Give my child self-discipline so that she can control her anger when it arises and have the right perspective on the situation. I pray that your Spirit will work in her and make her an effective and godly leader.

GOD'S PROMISE TO YOU

- When God places your child in a position of leadership, he will be with her.
- God can give your child a spirit of power, love, and self-discipline in order to lead effectively.

THE PROMISE
WE CAN CONFESS OUR SINS
AND RECEIVE MERCY

People who cover over their sins will not prosper. But if they confess and forsake them, they will receive mercy.

Proverbs 28:13

IT is difficult to admit our mistakes; it's hard to say we're wrong; it's *very* hard to say we're sorry. Yet we need to be people who do not constantly attempt to cover our sins. I don't know about you, but I get tired of people who always blame their problems on someone else. I've known a few in my day, and I react strongly against it when I catch my children doing it. I try to teach them to take responsibility for their actions and to admit when they are wrong.

Here in the Old Testament, the Bible tells us that covering up sin doesn't move us ahead. Instead, we'll spend so much time trying to remember what we said to whom that eventually we will get caught. How much better to be honest right from the start. How much better to confess and forsake wrongdoing. This verse says that we will receive mercy—from the ones we have wronged, we hope, but always from God. The New Testament promises, "If we confess our sins to him, he is faithful and just to forgive us and to cleanse us from every wrong" (1 John 1:9).

PRAYING GOD'S PROMISE

You say, Lord, that people who cover their sins will not prosper. When we confess and forsake our sins, we will receive mercy. Give my child the strength of character to take responsibility for his actions and not to blame others. I pray that he will be able to admit his wrongdoing and seek forgiveness from you and from the person he has wronged. I pray that my child will not only confess his sins but will also forsake them. You promise that when we confess our sins to you, you will forgive us and cleanse us. Draw my child back to you when he needs to seek forgiveness from you, and give him the assurance of your faithful mercy.

GOD'S PROMISE TO YOU

- When your child confesses and forsakes his sin, he will receive mercy.

THE PROMISE
GOD CALLS US TO DO GOOD WORKS

God saved you by his special favor when you believed. And
you can't take credit for this; it is a gift from God. Salvation is
not a reward for the good things we have done, so none of us
can boast about it. For we are God's masterpiece. He has
created us anew in Christ Jesus, so that we can do the good
things he planned for us long ago. Ephesians 2:8-10

OUR Christian lives should be characterized by good deeds. The
Bible makes it clear that good deeds cannot earn our salvation.
Salvation is a gift. But salvation makes us new people and gives
us new lives. God sees us as his masterpieces. As his new people,
we embark on a life of adventure. But we don't have to dash
around trying to find good things to do for God. Instead, those
good things were already planned out for us a long time ago.
We simply need to be obedient, and God will make them clear
to us. He will put certain people into our lives, bring us to the
right place at the right time, give us special abilities that he will
use, and give us a heart for meeting a certain need. God calls us
to do good works. What those good works will be depends on
where God leads us.

We can pray for our children to understand that they are
called to do good things for God. They should follow him in

obedience, knowing that every good deed they do is for God's glory.

PRAYING GOD'S PROMISE

What a glorious gift, Lord, that you saved us! We can take no credit for our salvation, for you gave it to us. I pray that my child will never be caught in the trap of thinking that she has to do good deeds in order to earn or hold onto your salvation. She is saved by your grace, and good deeds are simply part of your plan for her. You say that the good deeds we do have already been planned for us. Help my child to walk daily in obedience to you so that she will know the good deeds you have prepared. Thank you for the blessed opportunity to serve you and your kingdom in this way. Give my child the joy of service, and help her to always give you the glory for the good things she does.

GOD'S PROMISE TO YOU

- God saves your child not because she is good but because he chooses to show his favor to her.
- Your child is God's masterpiece. God makes her new in Christ Jesus so that she can do the good things he planned for her long ago.

THE PROMISE
GOD CALLS US TO USE OUR GIFTS

There are different kinds of spiritual gifts, but it is the same Holy Spirit who is the source of them all. There are different kinds of service in the church, but it is the same Lord we are serving. There are different ways God works in our lives, but it is the same God who does the work through all of us. A spiritual gift is given to each of us as a means of helping the entire church.   1 Corinthians 12:4-7

GOD graciously gives every believer at least one spiritual gift to use to build up the church. We cannot choose the gift we want; God decides (1 Corinthians 12:11). So it follows, then, that we must discover our gift and then use it for God's glory.

Paul made it clear that there are different kinds of gifts. The Bible gives some lists of gifts, but these are not meant to be exhaustive (1 Corinthians 12:8-10; Ephesians 4:7-12). We are to use these gifts in harmony with others' gifts so that the entire job of reaching people for Christ and building them up in the faith can be completed.

We need to pray that our children will discover their unique, individual gifts from God. This may take some time as they try out different things and finally discover what they really love and are good at. It may take some advice and perceptions from others. We can pray that we will be able to recognize our children's gifts and give them opportunities to use them. Then we can pray that they will use their gifts for God's glory and to bring others to him.

PRAYING GOD'S PROMISE

Lord, your Word says that you give your people special gifts that they can use to build your kingdom. Thank you for the different kinds of gifts, Lord, and thank you for giving them to each of us. This shows that every person's gift is needed in order to get the job done. I pray that my child will discover his special gift, Lord. You haven't stamped it on my child's forehead, so give me insight and discernment so that I can provide opportunities and wise advice. Give my child a sense of what you have called him to do for your kingdom. When he discovers his special giftedness, give him opportunities to use that gift. Help him to understand that sometimes his help will be needed even where he is not particularly gifted and that not being gifted in a particular area is not an excuse to avoid serving. Give him wisdom and discernment and many opportunities to use his gift from you throughout his life.

GOD'S PROMISE TO YOU

- God gives your child a special gift to use in helping to build his kingdom.

THE PROMISE
WE SHOULD NOT BE JUDGMENTAL

[Jesus said,] "Stop judging others, and you will not be judged. For others will treat you as you treat them. Whatever measure you use in judging others, it will be used to measure how you are judged."
Matthew 7:1-2

NOT long ago I heard a movie star quote these verses to back up her opinion that people should be tolerant of all kinds of aberrant behavior. Often, when Christians take a stand against sin, others throw these verses back in their faces. "Your own Bible says that you're not supposed to judge," they say with a sneer.

Today's verses do not negate the need for critical thinking or making discerning judgments. Other places in the New Testament tell us to expose false teaching, admonish others when they need it, and even exercise church discipline in cases of sinful behavior. Clearly we must make some judgments. The point is that we are not to have an attitude that is consistently condemning and critical, for that is not an attitude of love. We are not to attempt to take God's place as judge. It may seem like a fine line, but believers can take a stand against sin without being judgmental toward the sinners. God created them, and he loves them too.

Pray for our children not to have critical and judgmental attitudes. What a sad way to live! Christ has set us free to serve him with joy. Pray that our children will be discerning about sin without having a critical spirit.

PRAYING GOD'S PROMISE

Lord, you say that we are not to take your place in judging others, for that judgment will be turned back on us. I pray that my child will have a discerning spirit, one that is able to see sin for what it is and deal with it honestly and lovingly while not being critical and judgmental. I pray that judgmental attitudes will never harden my child's heart. I ask that when she takes a stand against sin, she will be able to do so with the loving spirit that you desire in your people.

GOD'S PROMISE TO YOU

● Your child can take a stand against sin without being judgmental and critical.

THE PROMISE
WE CAN ENJOY GOD'S GIFTS AND BE THANKFUL

Since everything God created is good, we should not reject any
of it. We may receive it gladly, with thankful hearts.

1 Timothy 4:4

HERE'S another couple of verses that people love to quote out
of context and make them mean what they don't mean. Some
try to say that "everything God created is good" means that
even sinful behavior can be acceptable because, well, God
created it, right? Wrong.

Paul was writing in response to false teachers who had added
many rules in order for people to be truly saved (specifically,
forbidding marriage and abstaining from certain foods, 1 Timothy 4:3). Paul explained that God created marriage and food
and both are good. Of course, people can abuse anything.
According to the Bible, God designed marriage to be between
one man and one woman. Homosexuality and adultery are not
what God planned and, therefore, are *not* good. God gave us
food to enjoy, but gluttony is an abuse of God's gift and *not*
good. Paul clarified that believers do not have to abstain from
God's good gifts in order to be saved. We should instead recognize God's hand in all the pleasures of his creation, use them
according to his guidelines, and be thankful.

Pray that our children will not forget that God gave them his gifts to enjoy. Pray that they will have an attitude of thank-fulness for all that God has given them.

PRAYING GOD'S PROMISE

Thank you for all the wonderful pleasures you created for us, Lord. Thank you for your beautiful creation, for wind, rain, and sunshine, for the joy of friendship, the intimacy of marriage, the enjoyment of good food, the excitement of adventure, the wonder in the eyes of our children. Oh Lord, let me never forget to thank you for all these joys. May my child understand from me that everything we have comes from your gracious hand. Let me thank you loud and often! You promise, Lord, that we can receive these things gladly, with thankful hearts. I pray that my child will understand that what you created is good when used within the guidelines you give in your Word. Let him receive these things gladly and with a thankful heart.

GOD'S PROMISE TO YOU

- Everything God created is good, and your child need not reject any of it in order to be saved.
- When your child uses God's gifts within God's guidelines, she can receive those pleasures gladly.

drown them. They can walk through the fire of oppression and not be burned up.

PRAYING GOD'S PROMISE

You promise, Lord, that when we go through deep waters and great trouble, you will be with us. Be with my child today. I know that she feels up to her neck in deep waters and doesn't know how to get out. I ask that she not depend on her own strength but will trust in your promise to be with her through this great trouble. When the river of difficulty is swiftly carrying my child, reach out your strong hand and draw her out. You promise that when we walk through the fire of oppression, we will not be burned up. When my child is in the fires of oppression and feels threatened from every side with no relief, I pray your promise that she will not be consumed by these flames but that you will protect and guide her through the fire.

GOD'S PROMISE TO YOU

- When your child is facing deep waters of trouble, rivers of difficulty, or fires of oppression, God will go with her through it, and she will not be harmed.

THE PROMISE
THE HOLY SPIRIT HELPS IN OUR DISTRESS

The Holy Spirit helps us in our distress. For we don't even know what we should pray for, nor how we should pray. But the Holy Spirit prays for us with groanings that cannot be expressed in words. And the Father who knows all hearts knows what the Spirit is saying, for the Spirit pleads for us believers in harmony with God's own will. And we know that God causes everything to work together for the good of those who love God and are called according to his purpose for them.

Romans 8:26-28

THE Holy Spirit helps us in our distress. In the middle of great pain, we often can't pray. We don't know what to say; we don't have the strength to muster the right words. So the precious Holy Spirit, who lives within us because we are believers in Christ, intercedes for us with God. He expresses our deepest groanings and pleads for us in line with God's will—because he knows God's will.

Not only are we promised the Spirit's help in our distress, we are also promised that everything that happens to us is working together for our good. The things that happen to us might not be "good," but God will make them work to our ultimate benefit, to help us become what he wants us to become—mature, Christlike, prepared for heaven. There may be suffering, pain, and trials, but under God's control, even these will be for our good.

The Holy Spirit will intercede for our children when their trials become so intense that they cannot find words to pray. God promises that his Spirit will plead in harmony with his will. God also promises that he will work all things together for our children's good. That's how much God loves our children.

PRAYING GOD'S PROMISE

Thank you for giving us your Holy Spirit, Lord. Thank you for his intercession for us when we are overwhelmed by trouble. Watch over my child today. Holy Spirit, intercede for my child if he cannot pray because the pain is too strong or the confusion too great. Express the deepest groanings of his heart, and plead for him in harmony with God's will. Thank you for calling my child to be yours. I pray that you will take this difficult situation and weave it into the tapestry of his life, revealing a beautiful design. I trust you to take even this distress and work it out for his good. I know that he may not be able to see it now, but help my child to trust that this is so.

GOD'S PROMISE TO YOU

- God's Holy Spirit can help your child in his distress. He can pray when your child can't.
- God can cause everything in your child's life to work together for his greatest good.

THE PROMISE
GOD STRENGTHENS OUR FAITH
THROUGH TRIALS

Be truly glad! There is wonderful joy ahead, even though it is necessary for you to endure many trials for a while. These trials are only to test your faith, to show that it is strong and pure. It is being tested as fire tests and purifies gold—and your faith is far more precious to God than mere gold. So if your faith remains strong after being tried by fiery trials, it will bring you much praise and glory and honor on the day when Jesus Christ is revealed to the whole world.   1 Peter 1:6-7

PETER says that we can be truly glad as we endure trials because of what we look forward to in heaven. Trials are not haphazard potshots that we're supposed to dodge; instead, they are opportunities for spiritual growth. They test our faith to see how strong it is. Do we hold on to our faith, without doubting, in the midst of trials? Do we seek God's guidance? Do we follow his instructions? Do we wait patiently for God to move, without whining and complaining? Do we stay close to God through it all? Sometimes we pass with flying colors; at other times, we need to fall on our knees in repentance. But in the end, as God strengthens our faith through trials, we will receive praise, glory, and honor.

Our children need to learn to rejoice no matter what trials

may be occurring in their lives. They don't need to be happy about the trials, but they can learn to be joyous in spite of them. We need to pray that as God tests their faith through the fiery furnace of trials, it will remain strong and bring them much praise, glory, and honor when Christ returns.

PRAYING GOD'S PROMISE

Lord, you promise that we can rejoice even in times of trial. During these times of trial, help my child to rejoice—not in the trial but in you, in her relationship with you, and in what you promise for the future, the "wonderful joy ahead." You say that trials test our faith, to show its strength and purity. As my child faces these tests, I pray that her faith will be strong and pure. I pray that it will remain strong after being tested and will be proven to be far more precious than gold. I ask that my child will be honored when you return, Lord, because she stood strong and rejoiced, even in the midst of trials.

GOD'S PROMISE TO YOU

- Your child can rejoice even in trials, for trials can strengthen her faith.
- Your child's faith is more precious to God than gold.
- If your child's faith remains strong through trials, she will receive praise, glory, and honor when Christ returns.

THE PROMISE
GOD HELPS US TO STAND FIRM

Use every piece of God's armor to resist the enemy in the time of evil, so that after the battle you will still be standing firm.

Ephesians 6:13

A BATTLE is raging—a battle that we can't see. The concept of spiritual warfare is difficult enough for me to comprehend, much less teach my children. They need to understand, however, that there are powers beyond our senses, beyond what we can see and hear. The Bible tells us that "we are not fighting against people made of flesh and blood, but against the evil rulers and authorities of the unseen world, against those mighty powers of darkness who rule this world, and against wicked spirits in the heavenly realms" (Ephesians 6:12). Pretty heavy stuff, huh? But it is true. The battles we wage in our lives are but part of a huge cosmic battle that has been going on since Satan's fall. This battle will not end until he is destroyed.

In the meantime, God promises that if we wear his armor, we can stand firm. As we pray God's promises for our children, we need to pray for strength in the unseen spiritual battles. We can dress our children in God's armor, just as surely as we would put on their shirts and tie their shoes. Over the next few days, we will pray for each piece of God's armor for our children.

PRAYING GOD'S PROMISE

Lord, I acknowledge that there is a spiritual battle being waged, a battle far beyond the scope of my senses. As a believer, my child is a part of that battle. I claim your promise, Lord, that as she wears the armor you provide, she will be able to resist the enemy in the time of evil and still be standing firm after the battle. Whatever battle my child is facing today, may your armor provide the protection she needs. Thank you for providing this armor, Lord.

GOD'S PROMISE TO YOU

- God can provide your child with his armor so that she can stand firm and resist the enemy in times of evil.

THE PROMISE
GOD GIVES US THE BELT OF TRUTH

Use every piece of God's armor to resist the enemy in the time of evil, so that after the battle you will still be standing firm. Stand your ground, putting on the sturdy belt of truth.

Ephesians 6:13-14

GOD promises that we can stand firm even in the heat of battle, but we need his armor. Today we will dress our children in the belt of truth.

A Roman soldier's belt was about six inches wide; it held together his clothing and provided a holding place for some of the other pieces of armor. The belt was the foundation of the soldier's armor, the first thing he had to put on. The foundation of the Christian's armor is the belt of truth. The truth of the gospel is the foundation of the Christian life. As we dress our children in the belt of truth, we are praying that they make the truth of God their foundation, the standard by which they measure everything else. We also are praying that they be truthful people who not only believe the truth but live it. We are praying that they be absolutely convinced of the truth of their faith, certain that Jesus is "the truth" (John 14:6).

Knowing and believing that their faith is the truth will help our children to stand strong against any enemy in any battle.

Many will attempt to make them doubt the truth, so tighten the belt of truth securely around their waists!

PRAYING GOD'S PROMISE

Lord, you promise that we can stand strong in any battle if we wear your armor. I pray that you will dress my child today with your sturdy belt of truth. So many people try to tell him that your Word is not true. Television shows, teachers at school, and other sources are vying for my child's attention. I pray that as I teach my child the truth and as your belt of truth rests securely around his waist, he will always come back to that foundation. May he always trust that you are "the way, the truth, and the life" (John 14:6).

GOD'S PROMISE TO YOU

- Your child will be able to stand his ground when he is wearing the sturdy belt of God's truth.

THE PROMISE
GOD GIVES US THE BODY ARMOR
OF RIGHTEOUSNESS

Use every piece of God's armor to resist the enemy in the time of evil, so that after the battle you will still be standing firm. Stand your ground, putting on . . . the body armor of God's righteousness.   Ephesians 6:13-14

T H E next piece of armor is called "the body armor of God's righteousness" ("the breastplate of righteousness" in some versions of the Bible). This body armor, or breastplate, protected the body from the neck to the thighs, often in the front and the back. It may have been made of leather, bronze, or chain mail. This piece protected the vital organs. No soldier went into battle without his body armor. Isaiah describes God as putting on "righteousness as his body armor" (Isaiah 59:17).

No Christian soldier should go into battle without wearing righteousness. As we dress our children with this body armor, we are reminding them that this righteousness is not their own but Christ's. As believers, they have been made righteous in God's eyes—in other words, right with God. This "rightness" gives them the ability to stand up to Satan's attacks when he tries to say they're not really Christians or that they're not "good enough" Christians. They can stand strong knowing that they have been saved by God's grace alone and that Satan is incapable of inflicting any damage on their "right standing" with God.

PRAYING GOD'S PROMISE

Lord, you promise strength for the battle when we wear your armor. Today I pray that you will dress my child in the body armor of your righteousness. Help her to hold on to the truth that you died for her. Help her to understand the price you paid to bring her to you. That price provided righteousness, right standing, with you. My child needs to know that nothing Satan does can inflict damage on her right standing with you. May this body armor protect her faith and help her to stand strong when the battle rages. As my child comprehends her righteous standing in your eyes, may she be strengthened and motivated to stay strong for you.

GOD'S PROMISE TO YOU

- Your child will be able to stand her ground when she is wearing the body armor of Christ's righteousness.

THE PROMISE
GOD GIVES US THE SHOES OF PEACE

Use every piece of God's armor to resist the enemy in the time
of evil, so that after the battle you will still be standing firm.
. . . For shoes, put on the peace that comes from the Good
News, so that you will be fully prepared.   Ephesians 6:13-15

N O W we need some shoes. How many times have you put on
your children's shoes, eagerly anticipating the day when they
could tie those shoes themselves? Roman soldiers had special
shoes that allowed ease of motion and yet protection for long
marches.

Believers need special shoes. We are praying to dress our children with the shoes described as "the peace that comes from the
Good News." When they put on these shoes, our children are
ready for any battle because they are completely at peace, knowing that they are already on the winning side. This is "God's
peace, which is far more wonderful than the human mind can
understand. His peace will guard your hearts and minds as you
live in Christ Jesus" (Philippians 4:7). When Satan tries to
disturb our children's peace with his temptations, troubles,
trials, or accusations, they will have on the shoes of peace that
comes from their trust in the Good News. That peace can over-
ride whatever Satan throws their way.

PRAYING GOD'S PROMISE

You have promised, Lord, that we can stand firm if we wear the right armor. Today I pray that you will dress my child in the shoes of peace. I praise you for giving your people the gift of peace. I pray that the peace that comes from the Good News—peace about the past, present, and future—would give my child a constant readiness to handle whatever comes. He can be fully prepared for battle when he has the peace of knowing that victory will always be his in Christ. Whenever Satan tries to disturb my child's inner peace, give him the ability to hold tightly to the peace that comes through your Good News.

GOD'S PROMISE TO YOU

- Your child will be able to stand firm and be fully prepared when he is wearing shoes that are the peace that comes from God's Good News.

THE PROMISE
GOD GIVES US THE SHIELD OF FAITH

Use every piece of God's armor to resist the enemy in the time
of evil, so that after the battle you will still be standing firm.
. . . In every battle you will need faith as your shield to stop
the fiery arrows aimed at you by Satan.   Ephesians 6:13, 16

IN combat a soldier's shield was invaluable. It protected him
from blows in hand-to-hand combat and shielded him when
flaming arrows flew down from enemy lines. Whatever came his
way, the soldier could hold up his shield and protect himself.

Believers need the shield of faith. Faith means total depen-
dence on God. Hebrews 11:1 says "What is faith? It is the confident assurance that what we hope for is going to happen. It is
the evidence of things we cannot yet see." Our children need the
shield of faith. Satan will shoot his fiery arrows of temptation,
doubt, fear, despair, accusation, or problems, and only strong
faith can deflect these arrows. With faith our children can trust
that God is in control, that he loves them, and that he is working out everything for their good. Such faith can quickly
quench Satan's flaming arrows.

PRAYING GOD'S PROMISE

Lord, you promise readiness for battle with your armor. Thank you, Lord, for the shield of faith. I pray that you will dress my child with a shield that will help her quench Satan's fiery arrows. I know, Lord, that my child will be faced with a constant barrage of fiery darts aimed at wounding her. Give her the shield of faith and teach her to use it to protect herself from whatever Satan sends her way. May your shield of faith always provide protection.

GOD'S PROMISE TO YOU

- Your child will be able to resist the enemy and stop the fiery arrows of Satan with the shield of faith.

THE PROMISE
GOD GIVES US THE HELMET OF SALVATION

Use every piece of God's armor to resist the enemy in the time
of evil, so that after the battle you will still be standing firm.
. . . Put on salvation as your helmet.   Ephesians 6:13, 17

A SOLDIER'S head was a very vulnerable spot, and so the armor
included a helmet. God says that his people are to include in
their armor the helmet of salvation. The prophet Isaiah
describes God as placing "the helmet of salvation on his head"
(Isaiah 59:17).

God saves us when we trust Christ as our Savior. We are
rescued from the bondage of sin and from an eternity separated
from God. "We are made right in God's sight when we trust in
Jesus Christ to take away our sins. And we all can be saved in
this same way, no matter who we are or what we have done"
(Romans 3:22). The helmet of salvation protects our children's
minds from the doubts that can so easily creep in and under-
mine their faith. Doubt can deal death blows to those not
protected by an assurance of salvation. When our children
know, beyond a doubt, that they are saved, they can handle any
adversity, question, or difficulty. That knowledge will protect
them like a helmet.

PRAYING GOD'S PROMISE

Lord, you give your people the helmet of salvation to protect us. Please place the helmet of salvation on my child's head. I pray that the assurance of his salvation will guard his thoughts and mind even as difficulties come and doubts attempt to creep in. May he always wear this helmet, secure in the knowledge of eternal salvation and protected from those who would attempt to destroy that hope. Thank you for your salvation. Assure my child that when he belongs to you, he can never be lost again.

GOD'S PROMISE TO YOU

- Your child will be able to stand firm in battle when he is wearing the helmet of salvation.

THE PROMISE
GOD GIVES US THE SWORD OF THE SPIRIT

Use every piece of God's armor to resist the enemy in the time
of evil, so that after the battle you will still be standing firm.
. . . Take the sword of the Spirit, which is the word of God.

Ephesians 6:13, 17

T H E soldier goes into battle well protected from attack, but his
job is also to do his share of attacking, so he needs a weapon.
Roman soldiers carried swords, most likely short swords
designed for hand-to-hand combat and probably double-edged,
meaning sharp on both sides. A soldier's sword was a deadly
weapon.

Believers also need an offensive weapon—and God gives it. He
tells us to take up the sword of the Spirit, his Word. When our
children know God's Word, they are prepared to answer Satan's
attacks as well as other people's doubts and questions. Satan
tried to tempt Jesus by misusing God's Word, but Jesus replied
to Satan by using God's Word correctly and defeated him
(Matthew 4:1-11). The Holy Spirit will help our children to
understand what they read in the Bible and to apply it correctly
in their lives. We must pray that our children will love God's
Word, study it, and be prepared to use it to send Satan fleeing
for cover.

PRAYING GOD'S PROMISE

Lord, you gave us a weapon to use in our battle against evil, and you promise that with it we can stand firm. Thank you for the Bible, Lord. I know it's difficult to read and understand sometimes, but I pray that you will help me to be a good example in my love for your Word. I pray that my child will learn to love it, read it, and study it. Please allow your Holy Spirit to enlighten my child's mind to understand what she reads and how it applies to her life today. May that sword be drawn and ready when Satan attacks with his twisted truths. Give her the wisdom to use your Word correctly. Through the pages of the Bible may she find understanding, grace, comfort, and guidance.

GOD'S PROMISE TO YOU

- Your child will be able to stand firm in the heat of the battle when she is carrying the sword of the Spirit, God's Word, in her mind and heart.

O U R children put so much trust in us. They trust that when they're sick, we'll give them what they need to feel better. When they get a scraped knee, they run to us, trusting that we'll know what to do. When my son's bike chain falls off, he goes to Dad, trusting that he has the tools and the know-how to do the job. When my daughter's math page is too difficult, she trusts that I can explain it—well, okay, sometimes trust can be misplaced!

We never misplace our trust when we trust in God, however. Throughout his Word, he promises that we can trust him. He is completely faithful, so we can count on him to do exactly what he says.

When our children place their trust in God, it is never misplaced. They can count on God's promises to them throughout their lives. Let's pray that our children will discover what it means to place their trust in God—for every area of their lives.

THE PROMISE
WE CAN TRUST GOD'S STRENGTH
IN OUR WEAKNESS

Each time [God] said, "My gracious favor is all you need. My power works best in your weakness." So now I am glad to boast about my weaknesses, so that the power of Christ may work through me.   2 Corinthians 12:9

P A U L was suffering. He had some kind of debilitation or chronic illness that he felt was hurting his effectiveness in ministry. He writes, "Three different times I begged the Lord to take it away" (2 Corinthians 12:8). But each time God's answer was no. In fact, God said that his power worked best through Paul's weakness. God's grace was enough to make Paul's ministry effective.

I remember finding this verse taped to a wall (in a bathroom stall, of all places) at college. I attended Houghton College in western New York, a Christian school where people do things like tape Bible verses to bathroom stalls. Anyway, as I embarked on a ministry to a hall of freshman girls, I remember one day feeling completely overwhelmed and inadequate for the job. Then I found this verse, taped where I couldn't miss it! God said to me, "You don't need perfection; you can't be and do everything; you can't meet every need. You be you, and I will work through you—weaknesses and all."

Our children need to know that God's gracious favor is all they need. God will work in and through them—weaknesses and all—to accomplish his will.

PRAYING GOD'S PROMISE

You promise, Lord, that your power works best in our weakness. Work in and through my child, weaknesses and all, Lord. I see his strengths and know that you will use them, but I also see his weaknesses. I claim your promise that even in my child's weaknesses you can work to further your kingdom. I'm thankful, Lord, that we don't have to be perfect in order to be useful to you. Thank you that my child can continue to grow and mature in you. Use him greatly. I pray that he will be glad to boast in his weaknesses because of your power. Help my child to trust in your strength.

GOD'S PROMISE TO YOU

- God's gracious favor is all your child needs.
- God can use your child's weaknesses for his glory.

THE PROMISE
WE CAN TRUST GOD'S STRENGTH
IN OUR WEARINESS

Have you never heard or understood? Don't you know that the Lord is the everlasting God, the Creator of all the earth? He never grows faint or weary. No one can measure the depths of his understanding. He gives power to those who are tired and worn out; he offers strength to the weak. Even youths will become exhausted, and young men will give up. But those who wait on the Lord will find new strength. They will fly high on wings like eagles. They will run and not grow weary. They will walk and not faint.   Isaiah 40:28-31

OFTEN I have wished that I didn't need eight hours of sleep every night. I could get so much done during an extra eight hours! When my children were all toddlers, I often felt that I spent the day following them around and needed the night to do everything else. But, alas, sleep was far too precious, and I usually plopped into bed at night, physically exhausted and leaving many things undone.

At other times we feel weak and can't go on. Spiritually battered and emotionally drained, we are "tired and worn out." To those of us faced with physical, spiritual, or emotional exhaustion, God offers strength. Everyone gets tired and exhausted—even "youths" and "young men," like our children!

But those who wait on the Lord, Isaiah said, will find new strength. This is strength that comes not from self-discipline or positive thinking but from God himself. We need to pray for our children, for they will surely face times when they are tired and worn out. Pray that they can learn to wait upon the Lord, for he promises eagles' wings—strength beyond what they themselves could supply.

PRAYING GOD'S PROMISE

Lord, you never grow faint or weary. No one can measure the depths of your understanding. You are never tired or unable to handle a problem. And you are watching over my child! Thank you. You promise to give power to those who are tired and worn out, strength to those who feel weak. When my child feels tired, weak, unable to move ahead, I want to let her know that there is help available. You promise, Lord, that those who wait upon you will find new strength. Help my child to take times of exhaustion as times of waiting upon you. Help her not to give in to the temptation to give up but to simply wait for your help from on high. Give my child new strength, Lord. After she waits on you, answer her prayers with eagle's wings that fly high. Help her to trust you to give her the strength to run and not grow weary, to walk and not faint.

GOD'S PROMISE TO YOU

- When your child is tired and worn out, God will give her power.
- When your child is weak, God will give her strength.
- When your child waits on God, she will find new strength.

THE PROMISE
WE CAN TRUST IN GOD'S FORGIVENESS

If we say we have no sin, we are only fooling ourselves
and refusing to accept the truth. But if we confess our sins
to him, he is faithful and just to forgive us and to cleanse
us from every wrong.   1 John 1:8-9

Is anything more precious than forgiveness? What a blessing
when, after we've really blown it with someone, we apologize
and hear that person say, "I forgive you." A weight is lifted from
us, and our relationship is restored.

Today's verses acknowledge the reality of sin. We have
sin—that's the truth. And at times we yield to our sinful nature.
Beyond our comprehension is the fact that God sees us as righteous because of his Son's death on our behalf, yet he knows
that we will not be truly righteous until we get to heaven. So in
the interim, God offers forgiveness. If we confess our sins, he is
faithful (he will do as he promises) and just (he can do it fairly
because Jesus already took our punishment) to forgive and to
cleanse us.

Our children will be blessed when they understand this
precious promise. They don't need to live their lives attempting
to attain some fashion of "sinlessness," for they will be fooling
only themselves. Instead, they can live to please God and,
when they mess up, they can come to God in confession. God

promises forgiveness and cleansing. His justice provides for the promise; his faithfulness guarantees it.

PRAYING GOD'S PROMISE

Lord, you say that if we claim to be sinless, we're only fooling ourselves. Our old nature still exists. You promise that when we confess our sins to you, you are faithful and just to forgive us and to cleanse us from every wrong. I pray that my child will come to you in confession and receive your forgiveness. Draw him close to you every day. Help him to understand that he doesn't need to keep a list of sins he needs to confess. Instead, give him an attitude of discernment and humility so that when he sins, he will know it and desire to be cleansed of it. Thank you for your forgiveness which removes sins as far as the east is from the west. Thank you for the promise of your forgiveness when we come to you. Help my child to trust in your forgiveness.

GOD'S PROMISE TO YOU

- When your child confesses his sins, God will be faithful and just and will forgive those sins and cleanse him from every wrong.

THE PROMISE
WE CAN TRUST IN GOD'S PROVISION

[Jesus said,] "Don't worry about having enough food or drink or clothing. Why be like the pagans who are so deeply concerned about these things? Your heavenly Father already knows all your needs, and he will give you all you need from day to day if you live for him and make the Kingdom of God your primary concern."

Matthew 6:31-33

Food, drink, and clothing are important. Add shelter to the list, and you have the basics for survival. God is not advocating homelessness; we must take care of these things. The key word is "worry." We are expected to provide the basics for ourselves and our families, but we should not *worry* about them. God will provide what we *need*. That is key. Sometimes people worry because they got in over their heads trying to get what they *wanted* (instead of simply what they *needed*).

Our children will need to learn responsibility. They will need to learn to provide for themselves and their families. They will need to hold a job and earn a living. But let's pray that they will infuse all of their pursuits and responsibilities with concern for God's kingdom. When that is their primary concern, then even as they work at their jobs or tend the home or cook meals or shop for clothing, they will have the right perspective. Pray that our children will honor, represent, and remember God at all times. And if the going gets tough for a time, they don't need to worry, for they can trust God to provide everything they need.

PRAYING GOD'S PROMISE

Lord, you tell us not to worry about having enough food, drink, or clothing. Give my child the right perspective on this, Lord. I pray that she will learn contentment. You know all of our needs and will give us all we need from day to day. Help my child to see that this is not a call to personal irresponsibility but a call to trust in you. Help her to see the difference between her needs and her wants. Remind her that everything she has is from your gracious hand. May she always give back a portion to you. She needs to live her life—have a job, provide for a family, pay bills—but doing all of this with your kingdom and its growth as her central concern will transform those responsibilities into an exciting adventure as she lives for you. Give my child such a transformed life, Lord.

GOD'S PROMISE TO YOU

- Your child does not need to worry about basic needs, for God already knows them and will provide.
- Your child can live a bountiful life—even in day-to-day activities—when she keeps the honor and glory of God's kingdom as her primary concern.

THE PROMISE
WE CAN TRUST IN GOD'S GRACE

Jesus said, "Come to me, all of you who are weary and carry heavy burdens, and I will give you rest. Take my yoke upon you. Let me teach you, because I am humble and gentle, and you will find rest for your souls. For my yoke fits perfectly, and the burden I give you is light."   Matthew 11:28-30

THE pious religious leaders of Jesus' day had burdened the Jewish people with many rules and regulations for living an "acceptable" life. Then along came Jesus, setting people free from the burdens of trying to be good enough for God. Jesus told the people to take off those burdens and pick up his yoke. There is still a yoke—following Jesus means commitment and sacrifice—but his yoke yields joy, fruitful service, and fulfillment.

There are a couple of extremes in the world today. Some believers want to take away other believers' freedom in Christ and replace it with a list of rules for how to live acceptably. These people are modern-day Pharisees. Others claim to be Christians but throw out all of the Bible's clear commands. The first group ignores grace; the second abuses it. In between stands Jesus, having set us free from bondage in order to take up his yoke of righteousness. We need to live the joyous life of grace before our children and teach them the joy that Christ gives. His burden is not meant to drag them down into shame or guilt but to make them contagious, thankful, joyous believers! Now that's a yoke that "fits perfectly"!

PRAYING GOD'S PROMISE

Thank you, Jesus, for setting us free from our burden of sin and our attempts at trying to be good enough for you. You paid the price—for us to try to do more is to say that your death wasn't sufficient. I pray that my child will never be burdened by legalistic rule keeping. I pray also that he will not go to the other extreme and ignore your clear commands. You say that your yoke is light and fits perfectly. To take up your yoke means commitment, effort, and sacrifice, but it leads to a life of fruitful service for you. I pray that my child will take up your yoke, Jesus. It frees him from the dead-end cycles of rule keeping, guilt, and trying to be good enough. It frees him to serve you wholeheartedly, courageously, joyfully. May he be that kind of servant for you, wearing your perfectly fitting yoke.

GOD'S PROMISE TO YOU

- Your child can come to Christ with his weariness and heavy burdens, and Christ will give him rest.
- He can take up Christ's yoke, for it fits perfectly and is light.

THE PROMISE
WE CAN TRUST IN THE POWER OF PRAYER

The earnest prayer of a righteous person has great power and wonderful results.   James 5:16

C A N prayer really make a difference? If God knows everything that's going to happen, why pray? Can we really change God's mind?

We might be tempted to live as though our lives are set and we must sit back and watch them happen. We have no control, so why try to do anything? I picture God as having to take his cosmic cattle prod and zap us into action. We are on this earth for a purpose—we need to get moving!

We know that God knows everything, that all our days are in his book and the hairs of our head are numbered. But *we* don't know everything, and our lives on this earth are a continuous quest of getting to know God better. So we talk to him, pray for guidance, ask for advice, seek help, plead for healing or protection. Does prayer change anything? Perhaps the better question is, Does prayer change us? The Bible promises that our earnest prayers have great power and wonderful results. So we must model this for our children and teach them to pray. Prayer changes things—but most of all, it changes us.

PRAYING GOD'S PROMISE

You say that the earnest prayer of a righteous person has great power and wonderful results. I realize, Lord, that this doesn't mean that you answer every prayer with an unequivocal yes. Instead, our prayers have power and yield results—maybe in ways we will never know. I ask that my child will grasp the awesome power of prayer. I pray that she will understand that it is part of her relationship with you, a matter of constant communication every day in every situation. Whether or not the prayer actually changes what happens is not the issue—the issue is that when we see prayer answered, we know that we have been heard. Give my child's prayers great power and wonderful results. I pray that she will see and experience that power even today, Lord. Let her know that you do hear her prayers and that you answer.

GOD'S PROMISE TO YOU

- Your child's prayers can have great power and wonderful results.

I'D LOVE to be able to shield my children from every problem, difficulty, or trial that comes their way. I can't bear it when they have to pay the consequences for a wrongdoing—but I have to learn to bear it because they must do so. Our children need to be able to learn from their mistakes. I can play a role in helping them to discern what the lesson is in a particular situation, but I am only guiding them so that someday they will be able to do that for themselves. When they make mistakes and God teaches them a lesson, they need to learn it.

God promises that he will discipline us when we need it. When our children face God's discipline, we must resist the urge to step in. Instead, we must let God work. Our children will be far better off when they learn God's lessons and learn from him how not to repeat the same mistakes!

THE PROMISE
GOD DISCIPLINES US BECAUSE
HE DELIGHTS IN US

My child, don't ignore it when the Lord disciplines you, and don't be discouraged when he corrects you. For the Lord corrects those he loves, just as a father corrects a child in whom he delights.

Proverbs 3:11-12

W E give the advice in these verses to our precious children when we discipline them. We certainly train them never to ignore us, and we also hope that they will not be discouraged by our discipline. Loving discipline teaches our children what is right while showing them that we discipline them because we love them. I have often told my sobbing children that I'm only trying to teach them what they will need to know in the future in order to be mature and to act correctly and responsibly. Even though it's hard for them to understand, I do so because I delight in them.

So it is with God. Like a loving father he disciplines us because he wants us to mature and to act correctly and responsibly. We would do well not to ignore him or be discouraged. He disciplines us because he delights in us.

We need to pray that our precious children will understand that our discipline comes because we care so very much about them. Pray that they will carry that understanding into the future when they may experience God's discipline. Pray that they will not be discouraged but, instead, see it as evidence that God delights in them.

PRAYING GOD'S PROMISE

Lord, you say that you correct your children because you love them and delight in them. I know what it's like to correct my child and to have to cause him pain in the process. I pray that he will understand that I discipline him because I delight in him and desire him to become mature. I ask that when he faces your discipline, he will also understand that you delight in him. Thank you, Lord, for being a loving Father who cares enough to teach us what is right by way of discipline. May my child never ignore your discipline or get discouraged. May he learn the lesson you have to teach. I pray that any discipline will result in maturity.

GOD'S PROMISE TO YOU

- God may discipline your child at times, but only because he is a loving Father who corrects a child in whom he delights.

THE PROMISE
GOD'S DISCIPLINE LEADS TO HOLINESS

Our earthly fathers disciplined us for a few years, doing the best they knew how. But God's discipline is always right and good for us because it means we will share in his holiness. No discipline is enjoyable while it is happening—it is painful! But afterward there will be a quiet harvest of right living for those who are trained in this way.   Hebrews 12:10-11

OUR earthly fathers (and mothers) disciplined us, and now we earthly parents discipline our own children. Often, however, our discipline is not perfect. I've been guilty of disciplining the wrong child or being too strict or too lenient or just letting things go at times because I'm too tired to deal with them! God's discipline, however, is always right and good for us. Today's promise is that God's discipline means we will share in his holiness. We already do because of our faith, but God is preparing us to be truly perfect in heaven!

Of course, discipline is not enjoyable—in fact, it is downright painful (if it weren't, we would never learn our lesson!). Precisely because it is painful, we want to avoid it the next time, so we try to learn what God wants and not mess up again. That's what the writer of Hebrews meant when he said that afterward there would be a quiet harvest of right living. We won't get straight A's in this life, but as we become holy, we are

SOME people subscribe to the notion that they live, then they die, and that's it. "Eat, drink, and be merry." Since there is nothing but this life, we might as well enjoy ourselves. In fact, who would want to be a Christian, then, and try to do good and live right? What would be the point? Paul wrote, "If there is no resurrection of the dead, then Christ has not been raised. And if Christ has not been raised, then your faith is useless. . . . And if we have hope in Christ only for this life, we are the most miserable people in the world" (1 Corinthians 15:16-17, 19).

But that is not the case. Our faith is not for this life only, because God has promised far more. Death is not the end; it is merely a doorway into eternity. God promises that as Christ was raised, so we will be raised. Paul went on, "The fact is that Christ has been raised from the dead. He has become the first of a great harvest of those who will be raised to life again" (1 Corinthians 15:20).

When our children accept God's promise of eternity on faith, they can have great confidence for the future. Nothing on this earth can stand against that kind of confidence!

THE PROMISE
THE HOLY SPIRIT GUARANTEES
FUTURE PROMISES

You also have heard the truth, the Good News that God saves you. And when you believed in Christ, he identified you as his own by giving you the Holy Spirit, whom he promised long ago. The Spirit is God's guarantee that he will give us everything he promised and that he has purchased us to be his own people. This is just one more reason for us to praise our glorious God.   Ephesians 1:13-14

W H O are the "you also" to whom Paul referred? This meant all non-Jews who had become believers. Christ came to die for everyone—not just Jews but Gentiles too. God had promised that through one of Abraham's descendants, "all the families of the earth will be blessed" (Genesis 12:3). Jesus fulfilled that promise when he opened the way of salvation to everyone. When we believed the Good News, God saved us! In that moment God gave us his Holy Spirit. The Bible tells us that the Holy Spirit is like a security deposit. The fact that we have the Holy Spirit means that all the rest of God's promises to us will come true.

God's promises about eternity are as certain as our salvation. There is no need to doubt what God says. While we may not understand everything or even agree on how the future is actually going to play out, we do agree that Jesus is coming back to take us to heaven to be with him forever.

Our children can have every confidence in God's promises for the future. The Holy Spirit in their lives, which had been promised long ago, testifies daily to the fact that all of God's other promises will also come true. With Paul, we can "praise our glorious God."

PRAYING GOD'S PROMISE

Thank you for the Good News that you save us, God. Thank you for giving us your Holy Spirit and identifying us as your own when we believe in you. I pray that my child will recognize that the presence of the Holy Spirit in her life is a guarantee that you will give her everything else you promise in your Word. I pray that she will have confidence in those promises. She doesn't need to understand how all of those promises will unfold. She does need confidence in the promise of eternity with you. May she praise you constantly for the glorious future you will give her.

GOD'S PROMISE TO YOU

- God gives your child his Holy Spirit as a guarantee that he will give her everything else he has promised.
- Your child can be confident in all of God's promises for the future.

THE PROMISE
GOD PROMISES RESURRECTION

The fact is that Christ has been raised from the dead. He has become the first of a great harvest of those who will be raised to life again.   1 Corinthians 15:20

JESUS rose from the dead. People may deny it, but it is a fact recorded in God's Word and verified by many people who saw him. It is a fact for which the disciples—and many believers across the centuries—gave their lives.

The promise is that because Christ was raised from the dead, so we will be raised. Jesus said to a weeping Martha at the tomb of Lazarus, "I am the resurrection and the life. Those who believe in me, even though they die like everyone else, will live again. They are given eternal life for believing in me and will never perish" (John 11:25-26).

Eternal life begins the moment we trust Jesus as our Savior, and then it carries us through our physical death and into our resurrection life in heaven with God. Death is not the end; it is merely the transition from this life into the glorious promised eternity.

When our children know Christ, they need not fear death. They may have experienced the sadness of losing loved ones. They may be facing our imminent death. They may be facing their own mortality through sickness. Pray that they can take comfort in the promise that as God's people pass from this life, we will be raised from the dead to be with Christ forever.

PRAYING GOD'S PROMISE

You were raised from the dead, Jesus, the first of many who will be raised. Because my child and I believe in you as our Savior, we are among "those who will be raised to life again." Death comes to us all, Lord, and it hurts. But you are the resurrection and the life. One day we will be raised to live in a glorious eternity with you. Give my child the comfort of knowing that death is merely a doorway into your arms.

GOD'S PROMISE TO YOU

- Christ rose from the dead, and he is the resurrection and the life.
- When your child believes in Christ, he will not perish but will have everlasting life.

THE PROMISE
GOD PROMISES A PRICELESS INHERITANCE

All honor to the God and Father of our Lord Jesus Christ, for it is by his boundless mercy that God has given us the privilege of being born again. Now we live with a wonderful expectation because Jesus Christ rose again from the dead. For God has reserved a priceless inheritance for his children. It is kept in heaven for you, pure and undefiled, beyond the reach of change and decay. And God, in his mighty power, will protect you until you receive this salvation, because you are trusting him. It will be revealed on the last day for all to see.   1 Peter 1:3-5

BELIEVERS have a "wonderful expectation." We can look forward to a "priceless inheritance" that God has reserved for his children. This expectation, this inheritance, is eternal life with God. When we receive Jesus Christ as our Savior, we enter into a personal relationship with God. Paul wrote, "We are God's children. And since we are his children, we will share his treasures—for everything God gives to his Son, Christ, is ours, too" (Romans 8:16-17).

Nothing can happen to this inheritance—we can't lose it, we can't forget about it, no one will tax it and diminish its value! It is safely in heaven awaiting our arrival. No matter what happens to us on earth, our inheritance is safe. It will remain pure and undefiled—even sin cannot touch it. Change and decay cannot cause it to disappear.

God promises to protect his people until we receive this inheritance. Our children's inheritance of eternal life is protected by God. The inheritance we give them will not last forever, but the inheritance God gives them is eternal.

PRAYING GOD'S PROMISE

It is because of your boundless mercy that we have the privilege of being born again. Thank you for giving my child that privilege. Thank you for your mercy to a sinful world. Thank you for giving your Son to die for us so that we could become your children. You promise that we can look forward to a priceless inheritance with you, an inheritance that is kept in heaven, pure and undefiled, beyond the reach of change and decay. Give my child confidence that you have reserved a priceless inheritance for her. Thank you that in your mighty power you will protect her until she receives it because she is trusting in you.

GOD'S PROMISE TO YOU

- God has reserved a priceless inheritance in heaven for his children.
- When your child believes in Christ, she is promised that inheritance.
- God will protect your child until she receives it.

THE PROMISE
GOD PROMISES THAT WE WILL BE LIKE HIM

Yes, dear friends, we are already God's children, and we can't even imagine what we will be like when Christ returns. But we do know that when he comes we will be like him, for we will see him as he really is. 1 John 3:2

WE are *already* God's children—not when we're good enough, not sometime in the future, not if we prove ourselves—now. Yet there's something more to come, something we cannot even imagine. When Christ returns, "we will be like him, for we will see him as he really is." We not only share in his family, in his blessings, in his inheritance, but we will also share in his glory.

This is a vision of what awaits us. We may not understand fully; we don't know what this means, but we do know that it is what we strive for. Even as we live our lives seeking to obey God and become more Christlike, we know that we cannot do it in this life. We will not be perfect until we see him as he really is. When he returns, we will look into the face of our Savior and become like him in his glory. Think of it: Christ will share his glory with us!

Our children can trust in this glorious future. No matter how many times they may trip and fall as they seek to grow in Christ, when they belong to him, their future is secure. One day they will be like him, for they will see him as he really is.

PRAYING GOD'S PROMISE

You say that we are your children, dear Lord. Thank you for that amazing privilege. Thank you for saving my child and making him your child. It would be enough just to be your children, but you give us even more. You promise that when Christ comes again, we will be like him, for we will see him as he really is. Give my child confidence in your promise, Lord. I pray that he will trust that one day he will be like you, for he will see you as you really are. May he await that day with eager anticipation.

GOD'S PROMISE TO YOU

- One day your child will share in Christ's glory.
- When he sees Christ, he will be like him.

THE PROMISE
GOD PROMISES TO MAKE ALL THINGS NEW

I heard a loud shout from the throne, saying, "Look, the home of God is now among his people! He will live with them, and they will be his people. God himself will be with them. He will remove all of their sorrows, and there will be no more death or sorrow or crying or pain. For the old world and its evils are gone forever." And the one sitting on the throne said, "Look, I am making all things new!" And then he said to me, "Write this down, for what I tell you is trustworthy and true."

Revelation 21:3-5

CAN you imagine heaven? What will it really be like to live with God? John tried his best to describe what apparently was indescribable. We may not understand it completely, but we can trust that heaven will be a place of perfect joy.

The promise that God will make his home with his people fulfills the longing expressed in the entire Bible. We want to see God; we long to be near him. His Holy Spirit gives us a taste of eternity with God, but one day God's home really will be among his people. God will live with us.

On that day everything will be perfect. There will be no more death or sorrow or crying or pain. The old world and its evils will be gone forever. God will make all things new.

Heaven is a very real place. Everyone who has believed on the

Lord Jesus Christ will be there, and it will be our home forever. The hymn "Amazing Grace" says, "When we've been there ten thousand years, bright shining as the sun, we've no less days to sing God's praise than when we'd first begun." What a glorious promise!

PRAYING GOD'S PROMISE

You promise, Lord, that you will one day make your home among your people. Thank you that my child is one of yours, Lord. Thank you that we will be able to be together forever in your home. You promise that you will make all things new, that the old evil world will be gone. You promise that this will be a place without death, sorrow, crying, or pain. Give my child comfort in knowing that this is what awaits her. Let her trust that this is a promise that will come true just as every other promise you have made comes true. Help her to be faithful to you until she arrives there. Thank you for the reality of heaven. It will last forever, and it is our future. Thank you, Lord.

GOD'S PROMISE TO YOU

- Christ will one day live among his people.
- In that new home, there will be no more death or sorrow or crying or pain.
- Christ will make all things new!

LINDA TAYLOR has been married to her husband, Tom, a financial advisor, for eighteen years. Their three children, Courtney, Tom, and Sean, were all born within thirty-three months, so Linda has been a busy—and praying—mom for many years!

Linda grew up in a military family and spent her high school years in Bonn, Germany. She received her B.A. in English and writing from Houghton College. In addition to her family responsibilities and her writing, Linda team teaches a women's Bible study and, with her husband, teaches a Sunday school class.

Linda has been working in her field for many years, having been part of the team that developed the best-selling *Life Application Bible*. She was also heavily involved in preparing the seventeen-volume Life Application Commentary series on the New Testament and is the author of *Does God Care If I Can't Pay My Bills?* Linda works on numerous other writing and editing projects through The Livingstone Corporation and Tyndale House Publishers.

She feels very fortunate to be able to stay at home with her children while continuing to hone her writing and editing skills—thanks to her trusty computer and e-mail. Her favorite pastime is reading, but she and her family will pack their bags and travel whenever the opportunity arises.

PRAYING GOD'S PROMISES SERIES